REAL WORLD DATA

GRAPHING POPULATION

Isabel Thomas

H **www.heinemann.co.uk/library**
Visit our website to find out more information about **Heinemann Library** books.

To order:
☎ Phone 44 (0) 1865 888066
▤ Send a fax to 44 (0) 1865 314091
▥ Visit the Heinemann Bookshop at www.heinemann.co.uk/library to browse our catalogue and order online.

Heinemann Library is an imprint of Pearson Education Limited, a company incorporated in England and Wales having its registered office at Edinburgh Gate, Harlow, Essex, CM20 2JE – Registered company number: 00872828 Heinemann Library is a registered trademark of Pearson Education Limited

Text ©Pearson Education Ltd 2009
First published in hardback in 2009
Paperback edition first published in 2009
The moral rights of the proprietor have been asserted.

Edited by Nancy Dickmann and Rachel Howells
Designed by Victoria Bevan and Geoff Ward
Original illustrations© Pearson Education Ltd
Illustrations by Geoff Ward
Picture research by Hannah Taylor
Originated by Modern Age
Printed and bound in China by Leo Paper Group

ISBN 978 0 431 02954 2 (hardback)
13 12 11 10 09
10 9 8 7 6 5 4 3 2 1

ISBN 978 0 431 02968 9 (paperback)
13 12 11 10 09
10 9 8 7 6 5 4 3 2 1

British Library Cataloguing in Publication Data
Thomas, Isabel,
Graphing population. - (Real world data)
304.6'0728
A full catalogue record for this book is available from the British Library.

Acknowledgements
We would like to thank the following for permission to reproduce photographs: ©Corbis pp. **4** (TWPhoto), **12** (John Henley), **14** (epa/Nic Bothma); ©Getty Images pp. **6** (Stone/Peter Beavis), **11** (AFP), **16** (AFP/Peter Parks), **18** (Time Life Pictures), **20** (Chris Jackson), **26** (AFP/Farjana K. Gohuly); ©Photolibrary.com p. **24** (Nordic Photos); ©Still Pictures p. **22** (Mark Edwards); ©TopFoto 2005 p. **8**.

Cover photograph of crowd of people, reproduced with permission of ©Getty Images (Stone).

The publishers would like to thank Harold Pratt for his assistance in the preparation of this book.

Every effort has been made to contact copyright holders of any material reproduced in this book. Any omissions will be rectified in subsequent printings if notice is given to the publishers.

Disclaimer
All the internet addresses (URLs) given in this book were valid at time of going to press. However, due to the dynamic nature of the Internet, some addresses may have changed, or sites may have changed or ceased to exist since publication. While the author and publishers regret any inconvenience this may cause readers, no responsibility for any such changes can be accepted by either the author or the publishers. It is recommended that adults supervise children on the Internet.

CONTENTS

Some words are printed in bold, **like this**. You can find out what they mean by looking in the glossary, on page 30.

COUNTING PEOPLE

The population of a place means all the people that live there. You can count the population of your class or the population of your street. You can find out the population of your town or country. You can even look at the population of the world.

The world's population includes every human being, from sports stars in Spain to teachers in Timbuktu. It would be impossible to count them all. Organizations that collect information about populations **estimate** that there are 6,625,000,000 (more than 6.6 billion) of us. The exact number is constantly changing as people are born and die.

Enormous numbers are needed to describe the world's population. Graphs and charts help us to make sense of these numbers.

Why population matters

By comparing populations now and in the past, we can find out how places are changing. Governments study population to help plan how many schools, hospitals, houses, and roads to build. Organizations such as the **United Nations** study population to help find out which communities might need help to feed or house everyone. Businesses study population to find out how many people might want to buy their goods. The study of population is called **demographics**.

Bar charts

A graph turns numbers into a picture, making them easier to understand. This bar chart shows the population of the world's biggest cities. The bar chart has a vertical axis (sometimes called the **y-axis**), showing the number of people. The horizontal axis (**x-axis**) shows the names of the cities. Each city has its own bar. The height of the bar shows how many people are in that city. You can compare the height of the bars quickly, without reading the numbers. Tokyo has the tallest bar, so it has the largest population.

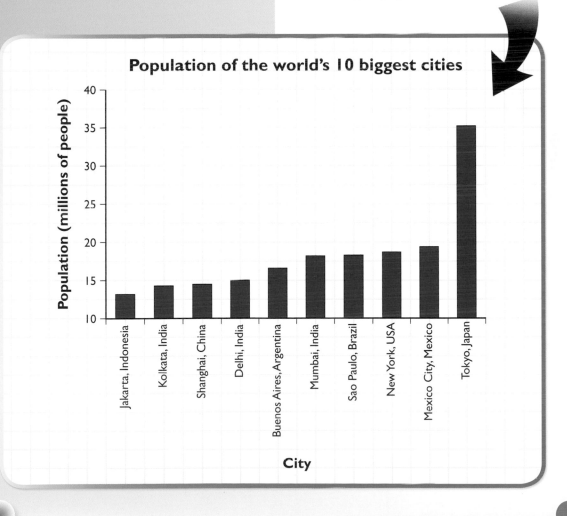

Population of the world's 10 biggest cities

COLLECTING POPULATION DATA

A **census** is an official count of everyone in a population. They are usually held every decade (10 years). The next UK census will be in 2011.

When governments carry out a census, they don't just count people. They collect many types of information, such as how old people are, where they live, and what job they do. All this information is called data. Governments and organizations study the data to find out where **resources** are needed, and to plan housing, education, health care, and transport.

Using a sample

One way to collect data (information) is by asking questions. This is called a **survey**. A census is the only survey of the whole population of a country. Most surveys use a smaller set of people called a **sample**. The people in the sample are chosen to represent all the different types of people found in the bigger population. This means the data collected from the sample tells us what a census might show. A sample is much quicker and easier to carry out than a census.

Members of a population may be very different from each other. Members of your class will have different heights and shoe sizes. They may speak different languages and live in different areas.

Frequency tables

A class carried out a survey of shoe sizes. They recorded the answers using **tallying**. One tally mark was made for each child. The tally marks in each row were added up to find the **frequency** (total number of responses). The data was used to draw a bar chart. The graph shows that most children in this sample have size four feet. Size four is the **mode** (the data that occurs most often). The smallest feet in the class were size one. Two children had size eight feet.

Shoe size	Tally	Frequency
1	I	1
2	II	2
3	IIII	4
4	HHH IIII	9
5	HHH	5
6	III	3
7	IIII	4
8	II	2

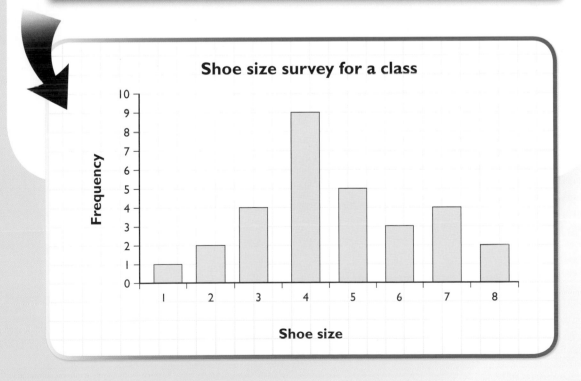

Shoe size survey for a class

Humans are thought to have lived on Earth for more than 50,000 years. For most of this time the world's population grew slowly. But in the last 200 years, the number of people has grown very quickly. Demographers call this a population "explosion".

The population explosion began in the 1800s. This was a time of great change in science and technology. New medicines and better **sanitation** meant that fewer people died of diseases. More babies survived to become adults. Farming and transport also improved, so more and better food was available. People lived for longer.

This picture shows the crowded slums of London in 1875. The population explosion was well advanced by then.

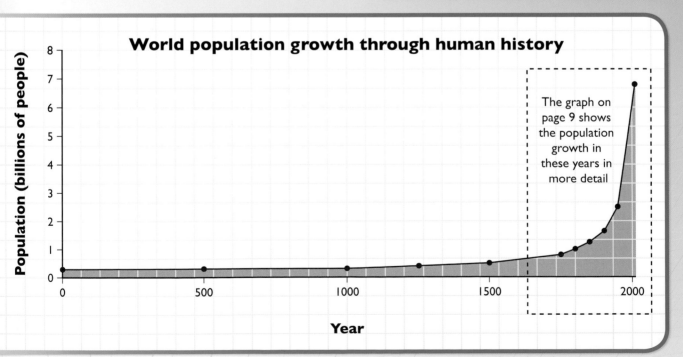

World population growth through human history

Population (billions of people)

Year

The graph on page 9 shows the population growth in these years in more detail

Line graphs

A line graph is a good way to show how data changes over time. Time is always shown on the **x-axis**. The population in each year is shown as a point (dot) instead of a bar. The points are joined together to make a line. The line rises up over time, showing that the population is increasing. The steeper the line, the faster population is growing. To understand a graph, read all the labels carefully. The label on the **y-axis** shows the units of measurement. On the graph on page 8, population is shown in billions. On the graph below, population is shown in millions. When you draw graphs, always label each axis and include the units.

Growing fast

The speed at which a population grows is called the growth rate. This is the increase in population each year compared to the original population.

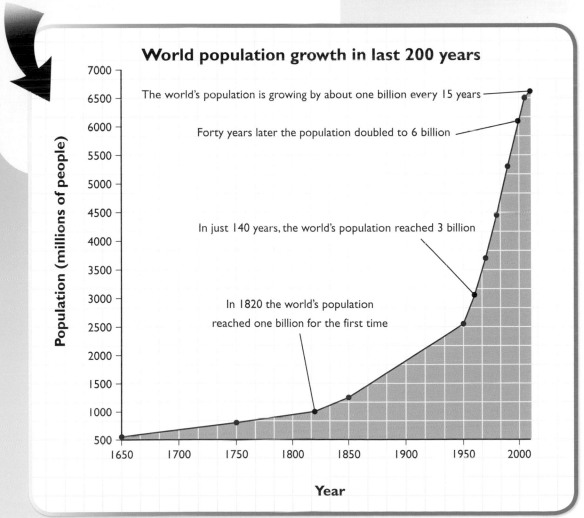

World population growth in last 200 years

- The world's population is growing by about one billion every 15 years
- Forty years later the population doubled to 6 billion
- In just 140 years, the world's population reached 3 billion
- In 1820 the world's population reached one billion for the first time

Population (millions of people)

Year

WHY HAS THE POPULATION GROWN?

Two main things affect the **growth rate** of a population:

1 the number of babies born each year (the **birth rate**)

2 the number of people that die each year (the **death rate**).

Births increase population, while deaths decrease population. When the birth rate is higher than the death rate, a population grows. In the past, many babies and children died at a young age. **Life expectancy** (the average age when people died) was low. Families had many children to make sure that some survived. Birth and death rates were both high.

Over time, death rates are falling around the world. Life expectancy is greater.

Birth rates are falling too, but not as quickly. The world's population is still growing. However, the growth rate is not the same around the world. Population is growing fastest in places such as India and Africa, where the birth rate is highest. In other places, population is growing slowly or not at all.

Different rates

In developing countries, there are about 3.3 births for each death. In developed countries, there are only about 1.6 births for each death.

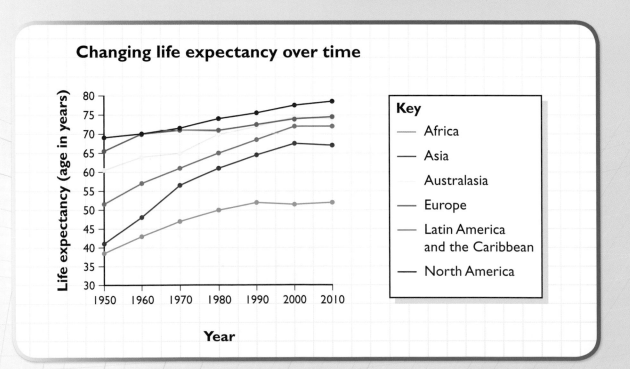

Changing life expectancy over time

Key
— Africa
— Asia
　 Australasia
— Europe
— Latin America and the Caribbean
— North America

In the past, **infant mortality** was high all around the world. Today, 943 out of every 1,000 babies survive their first year, because of advances in medical treatment. This newborn baby is being treated for polio.

Comparing data

Graphs help us to compare population data. This bar graph shows the birth and death rates for five countries. It does not show the total number of people that were born or died in each country. Instead, the graph shows the number of births and deaths per 1,000 people. This helps us to compare the rates quickly. It cancels out differences in population size between countries.

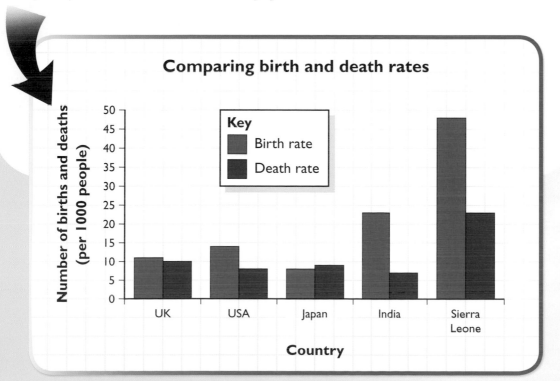

Comparing birth and death rates

Key
- Birth rate
- Death rate

Number of births and deaths (per 1000 people)

Country: UK, USA, Japan, India, Sierra Leone

The world's population is not just larger than it was in the past. It is different in other ways. As people live longer, there are more elderly people. Falling **birth rates** mean that there are fewer babies, children, and young people. On average, the population is aging.

Fifty years ago just 5 percent of the world's population was older than 65. Now the figure is 7 percent. More than a quarter of the population is expected to be older than 65 by 2050. The population has aged fastest in developed countries, where 14 percent of people are over 65.

 In developed countries there are more people aged 60 or over than there are 12–24 year olds.

Dependants

People under 15 and over 65 years old are sometimes called **dependants**. Most people in these age groups do not work, so they depend on people who do work for money and food. It is important that countries know what **proportion** of their population are dependants. The government must plan how these people will be supported.

Australia is a developed country where the average **life expectancy** is 81 years. Thirteen percent of the population is over 65 years old. Cameroon is a **developing country**. Its population is about the same size as Australia's, but the age distribution is very different. The average life expectancy is 50 years, and just 3 percent of people are over 65. Birth rates are high so there are many more young children.

Grouping data

These bar charts show the number of people in different age groups in Australia and Cameroon. The ages are grouped into bands of 10 years. Otherwise each bar chart would need more than 80 columns! Grouping data before you draw a graph is useful if there are many different types. The bars on these graphs go across instead of up, but you read them just like a regular bar chart – by looking carefully at the labels on the axes.

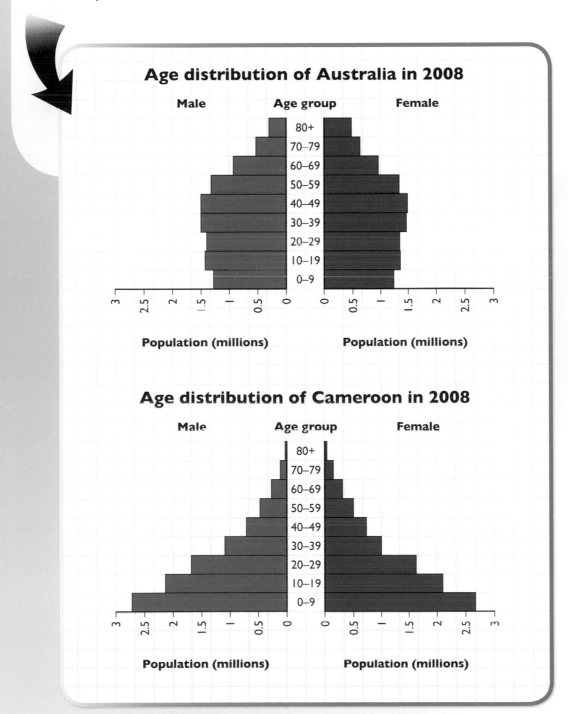

MIGRATION

Births and deaths are the only things that affect the world's population. They are the only ways that people can enter or leave the planet! However, a third factor can affect the population of a country or area: **migration**. This is the movement of people from one place to another.

People migrate for many different reasons. Some move to find work or to study, or because they think their life will be better in a different country. Others move to be closer to family or friends. Some migrants are forced to leave their homes to escape natural disasters, war, or other conflict. These people are called **refugees**. They do not have new homes to go to.

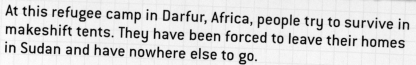
At this refugee camp in Darfur, Africa, people try to survive in makeshift tents. They have been forced to leave their homes in Sudan and have nowhere else to go.

The effects of migration

In countries with a low population or a low **birth rate**, **immigration** (the arrival of new people) can be an important source of new workers and skills. Many **developed countries**, such as the USA, Canada, and Australia have long histories of immigration. Immigrants from all around the world have influenced their cultures.

Migration can also have negative effects. There is a danger that immigrants are forced to take badly paid jobs and live in poor quality housing. Migration also affects the countries left behind. They may have fewer young workers to fill jobs and provide for **dependants**.

Multiple line graphs

More than one line graph can be drawn on the same axes. This makes them easier to compare. This graph shows us that migration has risen over time all around the world, but the number of migrants is higher in some regions than others. Europe and Asia have the highest immigrant populations.

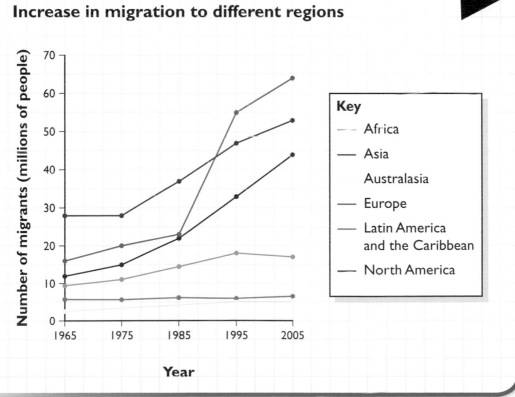

Increase in migration to different regions

Number of migrants (millions of people) vs Year

Key
- Africa
- Asia
- Australasia
- Europe
- Latin America and the Caribbean
- North America

As the world's population grows, a greater **proportion** of people are choosing to live in urban areas. These areas include towns, cities, and even bigger built-up areas. More than half of the world's population now live in urban areas, and a third live in cities.

Growing cities

Cities and towns grow when people move away from rural (countryside) areas. This is called internal **migration**. They may move to find work, to be closer to family or friends, or because they think their lives will be better in a city. The population of urban areas also grows as the people who move there start families of their own.

Urbanization is happening very quickly all around the world. Fifty years ago, 732 million people lived in urban areas. Now there are more than 3 billion. There will be an **estimated** 5 billion by 2030.

 Overcrowded transport systems are part of daily life in the world's biggest cities. This is the subway in Beijing, China.

There may be more work and entertainment available in cities, but so many people living in one place creates problems too. Around the world, one billion people live in overcrowded **slums** without clean water, **sanitation**, or proper shelter.

Pie charts

Pie charts help us to understand proportion (the size of a group of data compared to other groups). They show the data in different groups as different sized portions of a circle. Each of these circles represents the population of the world in that year. The larger a piece of pie is, the more people there are in that group. In 1950, most of the world's population lived in rural areas. In 2007, the proportion of people living in urban and rural areas was almost equal.

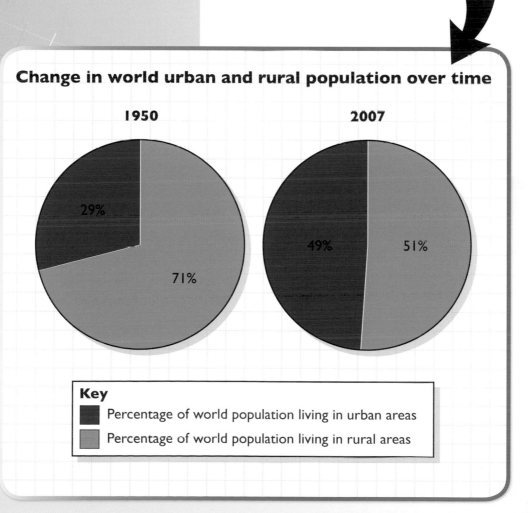

Change in world urban and rural population over time

1950

2007

29%

71%

49%

51%

Key

■ Percentage of world population living in urban areas

■ Percentage of world population living in rural areas

RICH AND POOR

All the things we take from the natural world, from food and water, to fuel and building materials, are known as **resources**. Just as people are not evenly distributed around the world, the world's resources are not evenly distributed between people.

Eighty percent of the world's income belongs to the one billion people in the developed world. The five billion people living in **developing countries** share the remaining 20 percent. More than one billion people are thought to live on less than $1 a day. This is extreme poverty. Poverty means being unable to afford the things needed for a good quality of life, such as shelter, education, food, and water.

A high population **growth rate** can be both a cause and an effect of poverty. As population grows, there are fewer resources to go round. People are more likely to suffer from hunger and disease. **Life expectancy** is lower, and **birth rates** are often higher. This leads to more population growth.

Some people have vast wealth, while almost three billion people live on less than $2 a day.

Unfair share

Europe and North America have just 16 percent of the world's population, but almost half of the world's national income.

Comparing pie charts

These pie charts show different data about regions of the world. Putting the data into pie charts makes it easier to understand. The first pie chart shows the **proportion** of the world's population living in each region. The second pie chart shows how the world's income is divided by region. If wealth were evenly distributed, the proportions in both pie charts would be the same. However, even though Europe and North America make up a small slice of the population pie, they have much bigger slices of the income pie.

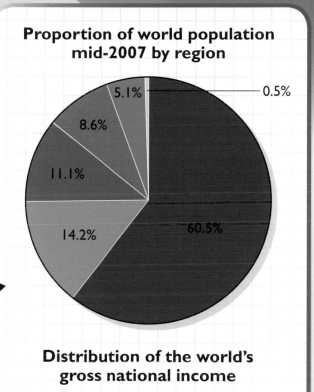

Proportion of world population mid-2007 by region

5.1%
0.5%
8.6%
11.1%
14.2%
60.5%

Distribution of the world's gross national income

3.6%
1.2%
7.4%
22.1%
40.2%
25.5%

Key

- Africa
- Asia
- Australasia
- North America
- Europe
- Central and South America

FEEDING THE WORLD

The first humans hunted or gathered all of their food. They followed herds of animals and lived in different places during the year. About 9,000 years ago people began to plant crops for food. This meant they could live in the same place all year – they were the very first farmers.

Most people grew their own food and lived near farmland. Populations grew quickly in areas near rivers, with good soil.

Over time, transport got better and food could be moved around countries and between countries. People no longer needed to live near farmland – but they had to earn money to buy food. Towns and cities began to grow as people moved there to find jobs. Today, cities can support millions of people. The food they eat is grown on huge farms, which are often in a different country.

▲ Around the world, two billion people do not get all the vitamins, minerals, and water that their bodies need.

Food for all?

Today's huge farms mean that the world could produce enough food for everyone. But food is not evenly distributed around the world. While families in **developed countries** throw away millions of tonnes of leftover food, 800 million people in **developing countries** are malnourished. They do not have money to buy enough food, or land to grow it on.

The **United Nations** says hunger and **malnutrition** are the world's biggest health risk. Anaemia is a condition caused by a poor diet. In some countries in Africa and Asia, more than 40 percent of young children suffer from this condition, which stops them from growing and developing properly.

Fertile farmland

Food can only be produced on 3 percent of the Earth's surface. Most places are too wet, too dry, too cold, too steep, or have too little soil for farming.

This bar chart shows the percentage of people who suffer from malnutrition in different areas of the world.

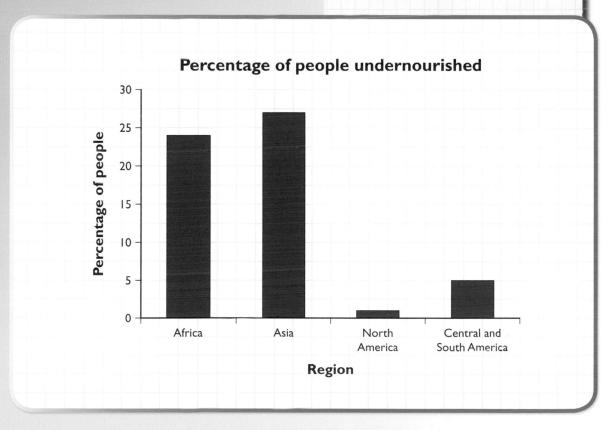

Percentage of people undernourished

DAMAGING THE PLANET

The world is becoming more crowded every year. Some places are much more crowded than others. In the wildernesses of Canada and Australia you could walk for many kilometres without meeting anyone. In one area of China, called the MACAO region, 20,246 people live in every square kilometre.

More people mean more demand for the Earth's natural **resources**. We dig up fossil fuels (coal, oil, and natural gas) and burn them to generate electricity and power vehicles. We use land to build homes and to farm crops and animals. We change the landscape by digging quarries and building motorways, car parks, dams, and electricity pylons. As we do all these things, we create waste that **pollutes** the land, water, and air.

As the world's population grows, the destruction of natural habitats is speeding up. This area of rainforest has been cleared to create farmland.

Two y-axes

This bar graph compares population in 10 countries with the amount of natural habitat remaining. There is a y-axis on each side. The red bars show the number of people on the left y-axis. The green bars show the percentage of natural habitat remaining on the right y-axis. The low red bars have high green bars next to them, showing that countries with lower populations usually have more natural land left.

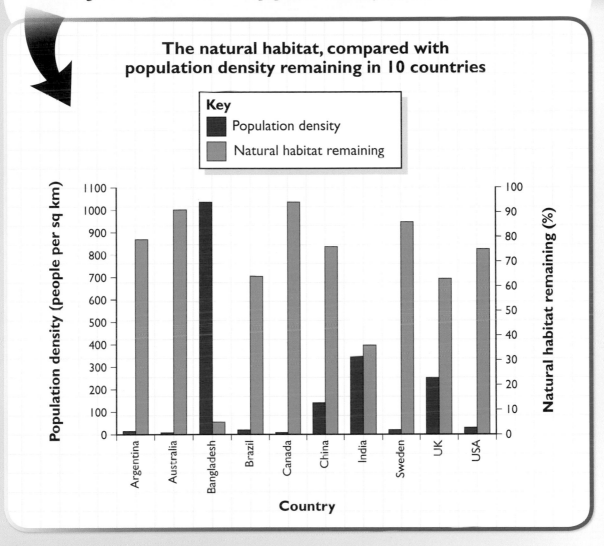

The natural habitat, compared with population density remaining in 10 countries

Key
- Population density
- Natural habitat remaining

Destroying forests

Ancient forests are some of the world's oldest natural areas. Rainforests are home to millions of different types of plants and animals, and help to control the world's weather and climate. About 8,000 years ago, forests covered almost half of the world's land. Now only one fifth of these forests are left. They have been cut down for wood, and to clear land for farming or building roads, settlements, mines, and plantations. As the world's population grows, the damage is speeding up. Every two seconds an area of forest big enough to cover a football pitch is cut down.

RUNNING OUT OF RESOURCES

Fossil fuels are **non-renewable resources**, and cannot be replaced once they are used. One day they will run out, but this is not the only problem. Burning fossil fuels releases damaging gases. Some of these gases **pollute** the air we breathe. Others, such as carbon dioxide, build up in the **atmosphere** like a blanket. They are causing the planet to warm up. This could lead to a rise in sea levels, flooding of towns and cities, and the spread of diseases, drought, and food shortages.

> We live in an energy hungry world, but our resources will run out if we keep using them in such huge amounts.

More people mean more energy use. But this does not mean that countries with the largest populations are most responsible for the problem. The USA and China produce the most carbon dioxide. However, China's population is much larger than the USA's population. The average person in the USA produces about five times more carbon dioxide than the average person in China.

Energy for travel
In 2005, more than 64 million new cars were built, and more fuel-guzzling aeroplane trips were made than ever before.

Telling the whole story

The same data can often be presented in different ways. By graphing information in different ways, you can find out the real story behind the data. It is easier to compare two graphs than two long lists of numbers. The first bar chart shows the total amount of carbon dioxide released into the atmosphere by eight countries. The second graph shows how much carbon dioxide is released per person in the same countries. You can see that countries such as Singapore, Australia, and the USA could do more to reduce the amount of energy that each person is using.

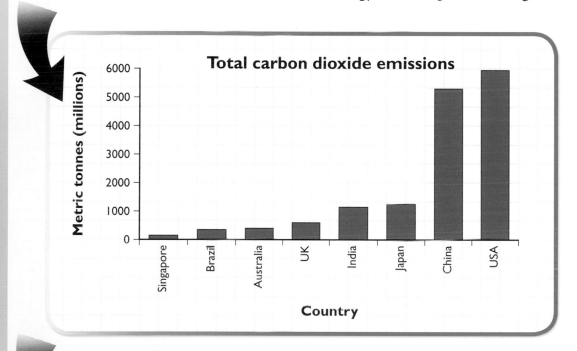

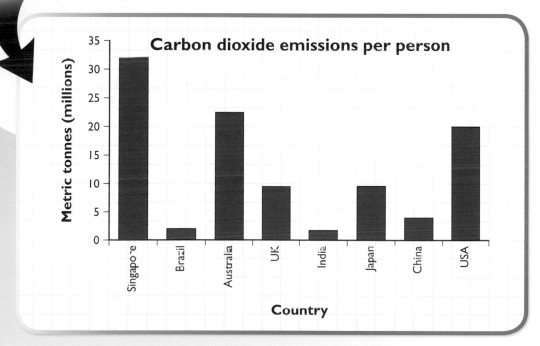

The world's population is already putting our planet under pressure. Some **non-renewable resources**, such as oil, are beginning to run out. The building of settlements, mines, roads, and farms has destroyed huge areas of natural habitat. Even the **atmosphere** has been **polluted** by human waste.

At the moment, the Earth does produce enough food, water, and other resources for everyone, but they are not evenly distributed. People in **developed countries** use far more resources than in other parts of the world.

> The more people there are, the more we affect the planet.

What next?

The world's population is still growing. Another 2.5 billion people could be living on the planet by 2050. This would take the population to more than 9 billion. The pressures on the Earth's resources and environment will get even bigger. Planning how to meet the needs of all these extra people must start now. It will involve **sustainable** development: using resources carefully and protecting the planet so it can support a large human population in the future.

New discoveries in science and technology, such as the development of **renewable energy** sources, may help to overcome some of the challenges of population growth. However, every member of the world's population shares responsibility for protecting the planet. If every person used fewer resources, used energy more efficiently, and cared for their local environment, 6.6 billion small actions would add up to make a huge difference to the future of our planet.

Making predictions

Demographers make predictions using international **census** data, and information on **birth rates**, **death rates**, and **migration**. This data is fed into a computer program that models how populations will grow. However, no person or computer can be certain what will happen in the future. Predictions are changed as birth rates change or events such as wars and diseases happen.

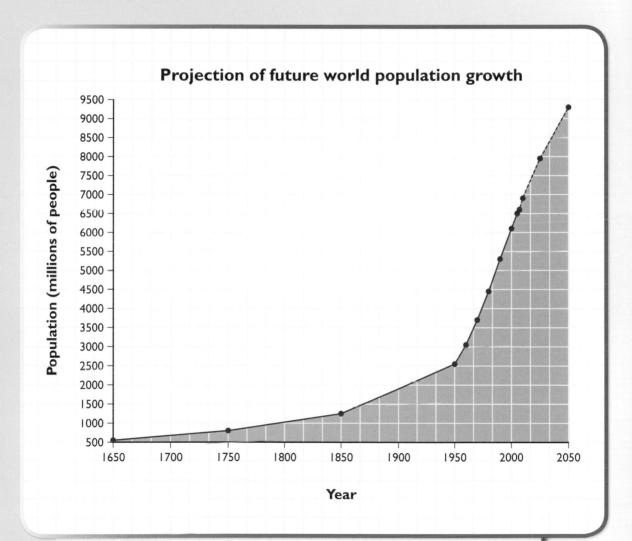

Projection of future world population growth

This line has been extended from the one on page nine to show how many people there may be in the future. The dotted line shows the predicted population growth.

Data is information about something. We often get important data as a mass of numbers, and it is difficult to make any sense of them. Graphs and charts are ways of displaying information visually. This helps us to see relationships and patterns in the data. Different types of graphs or charts are good for displaying different types of information.

Line graphs

Line graphs use lines to join up points on a graph. They can be used to show how data changes over time. Time is always shown on the **x-axis**. More than one line graph can be drawn on the same axes. This makes them easy to compare.

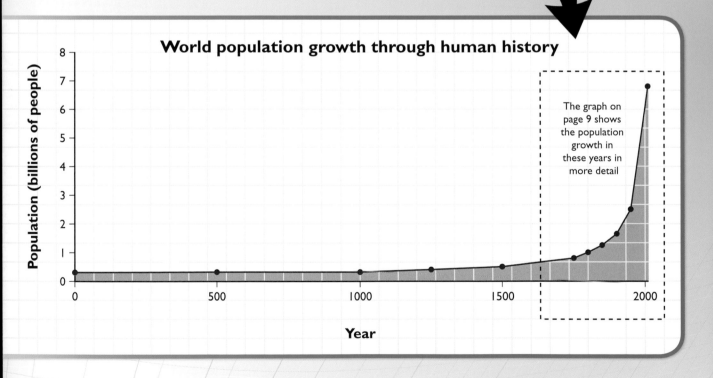

World population growth through human history

The graph on page 9 shows the population growth in these years in more detail

Pie charts

Pie charts show information as different sized portions of a circle. They can help you compare **proportions**. The whole circle shows the whole of the data. A large sector (piece of pie) means that a large proportion of data is in that group.

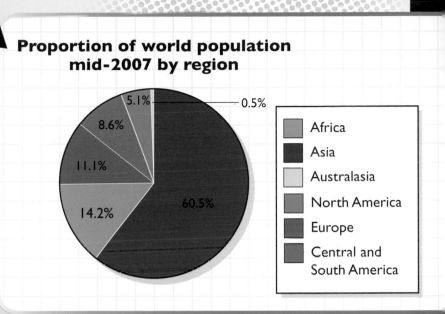

Proportion of world population mid-2007 by region

- Africa
- Asia
- Australasia
- North America
- Europe
- Central and South America

Bar graphs

These graphs are a good way to compare the results of a **survey** or an investigation. Bar charts have a **y-axis** showing **frequency**, and an x-axis showing the different types of information. When you are drawing graphs always label each axis and give your graph a title.

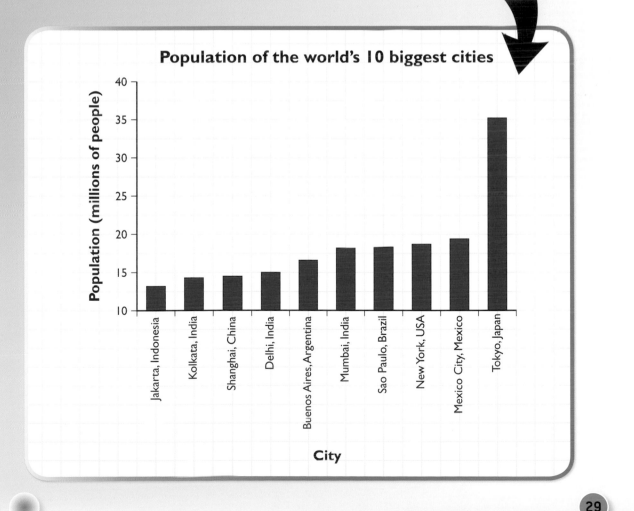

Population of the world's 10 biggest cities

GLOSSARY

atmosphere layer of gases around the Earth

birth rate number of babies born in a place each year

census when data is collected from every member of the population

death rate number of people that die in a place each year

demographics study of population

dependant young or old person who doesn't work so depends on other people for food and other resources

developed country country where many people are relatively well-off and work in offices or in new technology, rather than producing food or raw materials

developing country country where most people have little money and work either on farms or in industries producing raw materials

estimate number that is not exact but based on the data available

frequency number of things in a group of data

growth rate number of extra people in a population at the end of the year, compared to the original population

immigration when somebody moves into a country

infant mortality number of babies in a population that die before they are one, per 1,000 births

life expectancy average age at which people in a population die

malnutrition not getting the energy or nutrients needed for health, due to lack of food or an unbalanced diet

migration movement of people from one country or area to another

mode type of average; the most common, or popular, number in a set of data

non-renewable resource resource that can not be replaced and will one day run out, such as coal, oil, or natural gas

pollute make something dirty or contaminated with substances that wouldn't naturally be there

proportion size of one group of data compared to the whole set of data or to other groups

refugee someone who has been forced to leave his or her home but does not have a new home to go to

renewable energy source of energy, such as wind or solar energy, that will not run out

resource anything natural or man-made that is used by humans

sample part of the population from which information is collected in a survey

sanitation services like sewage and rubbish collection that keep a settlement hygienic and safe for people to live in

slum overcrowded urban area that lacks proper water supply, sanitation, or shelter

survey way of collecting information (data) by asking questions

sustainable will last and can be kept going over time

tally way of recording and counting data by hand as it is collected

United Nations an international organization set up in 1945 to work for peace and sustainable development around the world

x-axis horizontal line on a graph

y-axis vertical line on a graph

FURTHER INFORMATION

Books

If the World Were a Village, David J Smith and Shelagh Armstrong (A & C Black, 2004)

Planet Under Pressure: Population, Paul Mason (Raintree, 2006)

Talking Points: Immigration, Ruth Wilson (Stargazer Books, 2007)

Websites

Download a population clock and watch the world's population growing!
www.census.gov/ipc/www/idb/worldpopinfo.html

Find out about the history of the UK census.
www.statistics.gov.uk/census2001/ab_1.asp

United Nations Population Database is another great tool for finding detailed population data for any country in the world.
http://esa.un.org/unpp

Use the Datafinder at the US Population Reference Bureau to find detailed information about the world's population.
www.prb.org

INDEX